How Product Managers Can Sell More Of Their Product

Tips & Techniques For Product Managers To Better Understand How To Sell Their Product

"Practical, proven examples of how to make your customers want to buy your product"

Dr. Jim Anderson

Published by:
Blue Elephant Consulting
Tampa, Florida

Copyright © 2016 by Dr. Jim Anderson

All rights reserved. No part of this book may be reproduced of transmitted in any form or by any means, electronic or mechanical, including photocopying, recording or by any information storage and retrieval system without written permission of the publisher, except for inclusion of brief quotations in a review.

Printed in the United States of America

Library of Congress Control Number: 2016919227

ISBN-13: 978-1540415097
ISBN-10: 1540415090

Warning – Disclaimer

The purpose of this book is to educate and entertain. This book does not promise or guarantee that anyone following the ideas, tips, suggestions, techniques or strategies will be successful. The author, publisher and distributor(s) shall have neither liability nor responsibility to anyone with respect to any loss or damage caused, or alleged to be caused, directly or indirectly by the information contained in this book.

Recent Books By The Author

Product Management

- Product Development Lessons For Product Managers: How Product Managers Can Create Successful Products

- Customer Lessons For Product Managers: Techniques For Product Managers To Better Understand What Their Customers Really Want

Public Speaking

- Delivering Excellence: How To Give Presentations That Make A Difference: Presentation techniques that will transform a speech into a memorable event

- How To Rehearse In Order To Give The Perfect Speech: How to effectively rehearse your next speech to that your message be remembered forever!

CIO Skills

- What CIOs Need To Know In Order To Successfully Manage An IT Department: Decision Making Skills That Every CIO Needs To Have In Order To Be Able To Make The Right Choices

- How CIOs Can Make Innovation Happen: Tips And Techniques For CIOs To Use In Order To Make Innovation Happen In Their IT Department

IT Manager Skills

- Building The Perfect Team: What Staffing Skills Do IT Managers Need?: Tips And Techniques That IT Managers Can Use In Order To Correctly Staff Their Teams

- Secrets Of Effective Leadership For IT Managers: Tips And Techniques That IT Managers Can Use In Order To Develop Leadership Skills

Negotiating

- Use The Power Of Arguing To Win Your Next Negotiation: How To Develop The Skill Of Effective Arguing In A Negotiation In Order To Get The Best Possible Outcome

- Learn How To Signal In Your Next Negotiation: How To Develop The Skill Of Effective Signaling In A Negotiation In Order To Get The Best Possible Outcome

Miscellaneous

- How To Heal A Broken Leg – Fast!: Understanding how to deal with a broken leg in order to start walking again quickly

- How Software Defined Networking (SDN) Is Going To Change Your World Forever: The Revolution In Network Design And How It Affects

Note: See a complete list of books by Dr. Jim Anderson at the back of this book.

Acknowledgements

Any book like this one is the result of years of real-world work experience. In my over 25 years of working for 7 different firms, I have met countless fantastic people and I've been mentored by some truly exceptional ones. Although I've probably forgotten some of the people who made me the person that I am today, here is my attempt to finally give them the recognition that they so truly deserve:

- Thomas P. Anderson
- Art Puett
- Bobbi Marshall
- Bob Boggs

Dr. Jim Anderson

This book is dedicated to my family: Lori, Maddie, Nick, and Ben. None of this would have been possible without their constant love and support.

Thanks for always believing in me and providing me with the strength to always be willing to go out there and be my best for you.

Table Of Contents

How To Make Your Product A Success 8

About The Author 10

Chapter 1: Product Managers Want To Know: Should I Compete Or Create? 15

Chapter 2: Product Managers Who Want To Look Good Can Learn From Estee Lauder 19

Chapter 3: Here's What A Monster Truck Event Can Teach Product Managers 24

Chapter 4: What Product Managers Can Learn From Disney's Product Vault 30

Chapter 5: Which Forms Of Social Media Should Product Managers Be Involved In? 35

Chapter 6: How Can Product Managers Get Sales To Use Social Media Correctly? 39

Chapter 7: Product Managers Need To Know 4 Ways To Offer Their Customers A "Next Best Offer" 43

Chapter 8: How Product Managers Can Help Their Sales Teams Be More Successful 48

Chapter 9: Product Managers Need To Learn To Think Globally 52

Chapter 10: Product Managers Need To Know How To Find Customers In A Dark Room 56

Chapter 11: Let Apple Show Product Managers How To Sell More Products 60

Chapter 12: What Sequestration Means To Product Managers 65

How To Make Your Product A Success

How do you measure the success of a product manager? Ultimately it comes down to how successful their product is. The more units that get sold to customers who have decided that your product is what they really need, the better job you have done in creating a solution to your customer's problems.

As product managers we always need to understand where our next product is coming from. This means that we need to be able to decide if we want to jump into an existing market and compete with everyone else or if we want to try to create a new market for our product.

Getting customers to buy our product is a good first step, but how can we get them to buy even more? It turns out that the answer to this question can be found in a number of diverse places including at a monster truck rally or buried deep in Disney's vault.

Social media has arrived and seems to be everywhere these days. This means that product managers have to figure out how to use it in order to boost sales of their product. Once sold, we need to figure out how to work with our sales teams to offer our customers a "next best offer".

Where your next customer is going to be located is always a good question. Product managers need to start to think globally when it comes to selling their products. If we look around us, we may discover that companies like Apple are well positioned to show us how we can sell more products.

Since we can't predict the future, we need to always be preparing for the worst. There's always a chance that one of our customers could impose a sequestration and we'd have to determine the impact that would have on our product sales.

For more information on what it takes to be a great product manager, check out my blog, The Accidental Product Manager, at:

www.TheAccidentalPM.com

Good luck!

- Dr. Jim Anderson

About The Author

I must confess that I never set out to be a product manager. When I went to school, I studied Computer Science and thought that I'd get a nice job programming and that would be that. Well, at least part of that plan worked out!

My first job was working for Boeing on their F/A-18 fighter jet program. I spent my days programming fighter jet software in assembly language and I loved it. The U.S. government decided to save some money and went looking for other countries to sell this plane to. This put me into an unfamiliar role: I started to meet with foreign military officials in order to explain what my product did.

Time moved on and so did I. I found myself working for Siemens, the big German telecommunications company. They were making phone switches and selling them to the seven U.S. phone companies. The problem was that the switches were too complicated. Customers couldn't tell the difference between one complicated phone switch from another complicated phone switch.

The Siemens sales folks were in a bind. They didn't know enough about how the switches worked to tell their customers why they should buy them. Siemens reached out into their engineering unit looking for anyone who could help the sales teams out. I put my hand up and overnight I became a product manager.

Since then I've spent over 20 years working as a product manager for both big companies and startups. This has given me an opportunity to do everything that a product manager does many, many times. I know what works as well as what doesn't work.

I now live in Tampa Florida where I spend my time managing my consulting business, Blue Elephant Consulting, teaching college courses at the University of South Florida, and traveling to work with companies like yours to share the knowledge that I have about how product managers can make their product be a success.

I'm always available to answer questions and I can be reached at:

Dr. Jim Anderson
Blue Elephant Consulting
Email: jim@BlueElephantConsulting.com
Facebook: http://goo.gl/1TVoK
Web: www.BlueElephantConsulting.com

"Unforgettable communication skills that will set your ideas free..."

Create Products Your Customers Want At A Price That They Are Willing To Pay!

Dr. Jim Anderson is available to provide training and coaching on the two topics that are the most important to product managers everywhere: how do I create the products that my customers want and what should I price them at?

Dr. Anderson believes that in order to both learn and remember what he says, product managers need to laugh. Each one of his speeches is full of fun and humor so that what he says "sticks" with everyone.

Dr. Anderson's Product Management Training Includes:

1. How can you segment your market?
2. What problems are your customers having right now?
3. Which of your customer's problems does your product solve?
4. How much of this problem does your product solve?
5. How much will it cost your customer if they don't fix this problem?

Dr. Jim Anderson presents over 100 speeches per year. To invite Dr. Anderson to speak at your event, contact him at:

Phone: 813-418-6970 or
Email: jim@BlueElephantConsulting.com

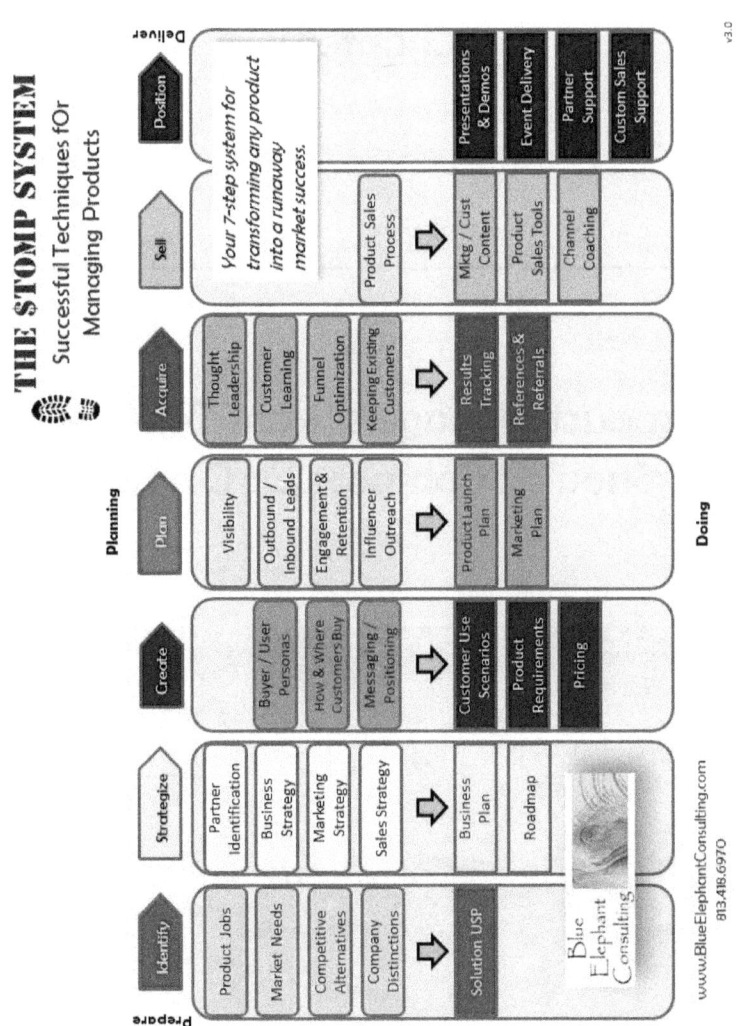

The **$TOMP** product management system has been created by **Blue Elephant Consulting** to help product managers know what to do and when to do it in order for a product to be successful. Contact us for more information on how you can learn more.

Chapter 1

Product Managers Want To Know: Should I Compete Or Create?

Chapter 1: Product Managers Want To Know: Should I Compete Or Create?

In the world of product management, there are a few **"classic questions"**. We all need to be aware of these questions because they keep coming up over and over again during our careers. One such question has to do with what type of market you should plan on selling your product to: an existing market or a new one that you create all by yourself...

Say Hello To Mr. Porter

In the traditional world of product management, we expect to sell our product **in a market that already exists**. This means that as Mr. Porter told all of us back in school, there will be 5 forces at work in that market.

One of these forces will be competitors. This means that we're going to have to spend some time coming up with a plan to make our product **distinguish itself from the competition**. All in all, this is what most product managers are trained to deal with.

Ready For A Blue Ocean Anyone?

In the past few years, **a different approach to marketing** has shown up. This was probably best captured in the book ***Blue Ocean Strategy***. Effectively what this approach is all about is deciding not to compete with other firms and products and instead going out and creating your own market.

What makes this such a powerful approach is that by doing this, you basically **don't have to worry about any competition** until other firms realize what you are up to and start to show up to compete against you. This isn't easy to do, but if done correctly can be a powerful approach.

Which Approach Is Best?

So here's **the big question**: which way is best for a product manager and your product? It turns out that we're going to get some help here. Dr. Andrew Burke and a team of researchers have been looking into this very issue.

The question that they have been trying to answer is whether a competitive or an innovative strategy will result in **the most successful product**. Their thinking was that if you pursued a "Blue Ocean" type of strategy then you'd end up creating a new market. Naturally, this market would quickly attract other firms. If as this happened, your product's profitability went down as more and more firms entered your market, then you'd know that the new opportunities for your product were probably limited over time.

What The Researchers Found

The researchers found that, not surprisingly, over time competition tends to **erode the profits** that a product manager may have been able to initially make from introducing an innovative product. If there is any good news in this, it's that this erosion takes time. Specifically it takes about 15 years.

What this means for a product manager is that taking a blue ocean approach and creating new markets for your product **may yield the best results**. You can't rest on those results because eventually the rest of the world will catch up with you, but you should have enough time to make generous profits.

The researchers suggest an even better approach. They recommend **a two pronged approach**: creating new markets while at the same time competing in existing markets. This will generate money from competitive markets that can then be used to find and enter more new blue ocean opportunities.

What All Of This Means For You

Product managers need to make important decisions as to what **types of markets** they want to introduce their products into. Two of the most obvious choices include entering competitive markets or creating new markets for your product.

Researchers have taken a look at the benefits and drawbacks of **entering each of these markets**. What they've found is that competition will eventually wear away at your product's profits. This means that creating new markets for your products buys you the most time to make the most profit.

Every product manager will need to make the market entry decision that **best meets the needs** of his or her product and company. However, taking the time to find new untapped markets can yield the best long-term bottom-line results.

Chapter 2

Product Managers Who Want To Look Good Can Learn From Estee Lauder

Chapter 2: Product Managers Who Want To Look Good Can Learn From Estee Lauder

As a guy, what I know about women's make-up can pretty much be written on one side of a file card. With a lot of space left over. However, as a consultant to lots of product managers, **I've always been very impressed by cosmetics products**. They are a simple product that a lot of advertising makes seem very valuable. It turns out that the long global recession has hit cosmetics companies hard also and so their product managers are doing something about it – they are changing how they sell their products...

How Make Up Gets Sold Today

Cosmetics is a big, big business. I'm not sure how large the market that your product plays in is, but **the U.S. beauty market is a $58.8 billion (yes, that's billion) market**. However, the global recession knocked about 9% out of this market last year and so the product managers are starting to scramble.

It turns out that 1/3 of a cosmetics company's revenues come from the products that are sold at **department stores** (remember them?) This has always been a great place to sell make up; however, times are changing.

Big Changes Are Coming To The World Of Make Up

Competitors are starting to show up. This competition is coming from both cheaper brands that you can find at drugstores as well as niche brands that are getting big marketing pushes.

As though that wasn't enough, the customers who buy make up are also changing. **Younger customers** really don't like the way that make up has traditionally be sold at the big department stores. There you have to wait in line for a "consultant" who then tries to up-sell you on many other products. Oh, and the price of everything is hidden – you have to ask to find out how much things cost. This doesn't set well with the young women who make up much of the market these days.

Estee Lauder's New Plan

Estee Lauder is a company with three major brands that you may recognize: Clinique, Estee Lauder, and MAC (I even recognize the brands!) Their product managers have decided that they need to change how their products are **sold in department stores** if they want to have any hope of remaining relevant in the future.

First things first – to make changes in how your product is sold in a department store, **you need the store's cooperation**. In the past, making a major change in a set of products that is one of the most profitable parts of a department store would create a lot of resistance from the department store. However, thanks to the recession, the department stores realize that something has got to change and are willing to play ball.

So here's a fun fact for you: 80% of the women who use mascara replace it at least 2-3 times a year according to a survey done by the NPD Group. When it comes time to replace their makeup, the younger customers really **want to touch and**

play with the makeup products. Estee Lauder product managers realize this and so they are redesigning how make up products are presented in the department store: customer now have easy access to the products and they can try them on before making a decision.

Time is a precious resource for all of us. The Estee Lauder product managers have come to realize that they need to **make the shopping experience different** for customers who have different amounts of available time. They've added an "express lane" to their displays so that women who know what they want can get in and get out quickly. They also offer areas where women can browse the different products and, for the customers who want it, they offer an area where customers who want a full beauty consultation can settle in for a visit.

What All Of This Means For You

As product managers we all wish that our product was as highly desired as women's make up is. Even if we don't work in this market, **we can still learn a lot** from the changes that the Estee Lauder product managers are making to how their products get sold.

As the characteristics of our customer base changes (e.g. they get younger), **we need to adapt to how they want to shop for our product.** The way that we used to do things may no longer work. Estee Lauder's product managers have discovered that their customers want to be able to touch and play with their products instead of having company employees hovering over them all of the time. Additionally, respecting how much time our customers have could make it easier for them to buy from us.

Watching what Estee Lauder does and learning from their actions can go a long way in **helping product managers better meet their customer's needs**. Take some of the same actions and who knows, your products might come out of this looking even better than they do today...!

Chapter 3

Here's What A Monster Truck Event Can Teach Product Managers

Chapter 3: Here's What A Monster Truck Event Can Teach Product Managers

Lessons in how to be a better product manager can come from the strangest places – including **a Monster Truck event**. I'm willing to confess, I dived deep into my redneck past over a recent weekend and took the family to the Monster Truck Jam event that was being held down at the local football stadium. Little did I know that I was going to get a lesson in product management...

Just What Is A Monster Truck Event?

What's that you say? You've never heard of a Monster Truck event? Well let me tell you what you've been missing! Essentially what we're talking about here is **a truck freak show**. Take a truck, pull off its tires, put on some very, very large tires and change out its suspension and vola, you've got a Monster Truck.

At these events, the Monster Trucks race each other to see who can make it around the track the quickest with **trips off of jump ramps** being part of the track, of course. After that's all done, now comes the freestyle part of the competition. This involves 90 seconds of driving the truck around and crushing cars and making jumps far into the air.

As you can well imagine, **this is a great deal of fun for the audience to watch** and the 60,000 fans that were in the stadium with me spent most of their time on their feet cheering for their favorite drivers and trucks.

It's Always About Your Next Sale

As a simple product manager surrounded by this chaos, I was stuck by the truly masterful amount of product management that was happening right before my very eyes. I quickly realized that there was **a lot that I could learn just by paying attention.**

One of the first things that I noticed was that the announcer almost from the start was **trying to get me to buy tickets to upcoming Monster Truck events**. It dawned on me that I had already self-selected myself as an interested potential customer for their next event by buying a ticket to this event. Me and my 60,000 friends were the primary target market for selling tickets to the next event and the Monster Truck Jam product managers weren't going to miss a beat in marketing their next product to us.

They were actually offering us **three separate follow-on products**. One was the opportunity to purchase tickets to the next event which would be the "Superbowl" of Monster Truck events that will be held out in Las Vegas. The next was an opportunity to buy tickets to a motorcross event that was going to be held in a nearby town in about a month ("if you like Monster Trucks, then of course you'd like motorcross..."). Finally, the third offer was for tickets to the next two events that are going to be held in my hometown of Tampa Florida next year.

The ticket purchase offers were **a constant theme** from the announcer and as he interviewed each of the Monster Truck drivers, they too invited their loyal fans to go out and purchase tickets to all of these events. Clearly the product managers were playing on the excitement of being at this event ("hey dad, can we go to the next event?") and trying to get everyone to buy their next product.

Make It Easy To Buy From You

Just having another product to sell to your customer and identifying who that customer is may not be enough. You'd like to take this one step further and make sure that your customer buys from you. To do this, **you've got to make it easy for your customer to buy your product.**

All too often we product managers spend our time creating the greatest product that the world has ever seen. We then proceed to drop the ball and don't do the extra work to make sure that our company's ordering systems are **easy for our customers to use** when they want to buy our product.

The Monster Truck Jam product managers had this all figured out. They had included a US$10 discount coupon in the program guide that all of the loyal Monster Truck fans had bought. This coupon would expire in a week so they had put **a sense of urgency into their fans** who were considering purchasing tickets.

They had also decided that directing fans to **purchase tickets online** was the best way to pre-sell tickets for an event that the normal Ticketmaster channel was not yet set up to handle (since the event would be held next year).

To build up **a sense of privilege**, the announcer kept reminding the audience that online ticket sales would become available at 11pm that night. He also pointed out that if you wanted up close seats, you needed to be among the first to buy tickets.

The event wrapped up at about 9:30pm and so the product managers had correctly guessed that a lot of the audience would be at home and still up at 11pm. They had cleverly realized that fresh from a fun Monster Truck event, they might **be primed to go online and purchase tickets** if they thought that by doing so they could get the best seats available. Those Monster Truck product managers really knew their stuff...

What All Of This Means For You

If you've ever dreamed of pulling off your car's tires and replacing them with 6 foot (1.83 meters) tires, then **you are a prime candidate** for attending a Monster Truck event when it comes to your town – and it will. If you do attend this event, you'll see some amazing things and you'll get a lesson in product management.

While you are at the event, you'll be constantly reminded about **other products that you can purchase**. From remote control spinoff toys to tickets to the next big event, the producers realize that since you've bought tickets to this event, you are a prime candidate to buy more products from them.

In order to convince you to shell out even more cash, the folks who want to sell you more stuff **make it very easy to buy from them**. They also encourage you to do so quickly – buy now and get the good seats, buy now and save money off your next purchase!

No matter what you think about Monster Trucks (talk to my wife if you shudder at the thought of attending one of these events), you've got to admit that **they are popular**. As product managers we can only hope that our products will be that popular someday. We need to keep an eye on these Monster Trucks and let them show us the way to better product management techniques...

Chapter 4

What Product Managers Can Learn From Disney's Product Vault

Chapter 4: What Product Managers Can Learn From Disney's Product Vault

Have you heard about the Disney product vault? This is the place that they put their products every so often. What this means for their customers is that they had better buy their products now because once they go into the vault you don't know when they'll come back out. Is this a technique that we product managers can use to **prevent our customers from going with the competition** or is it an idea whose time has come and gone?

How The Disney Vault Works

Does Disney actually **have a vault** somewhere in the ground where they put all of the unsold copies of movies like Snow White, Pinocchio, and Fantasia? Umm, no – this is just a marketing move by the mouse.

The folks in marketing organizations the world over have learned that when there is a real or perceived shortage of a product, people are willing to buy more of it and buy it right now! If you live anywhere where bad weather can strike you've seen this a lot: when that forecast of bad weather first starts to show up on TV, it seems like everyone goes out and **buys gas** and starts to stock up on bottled water before it's all gone.

Disney is trying to cause the same thing to happen; however, in this case **there is no impending natural disaster**. The only thing that is going to happen is that the product managers at Disney are planning on taking some of the products that they are currently selling off of the market.

The thought is that Disney will get **a double boost to sales here**. First, they'll get an uptick in sales as they tell everyone that time is running out to purchase these products. Then, when they announce that the products are "coming out of the vault" they'll get another boost as customers rush to buy what was previously not available. How's that for a great business model?

Why The Disney Vault May No Longer Be A Good Idea

This concept of a **"product vault"** may have worked for Disney and others in the past, but does it still work? Maybe, but not nearly as much as it once did. In order for a product vault concept to work, you really have to be able to make your product leave the market.

The problem with this is that here in the 21st Century, that's really hard to do. In fact, if your product is **a digital product** like Disney's is, it's nigh impossible to do.

Case in point: the movie Fantasia. Let's say that Disney announces that they're putting this product into the vault tomorrow. Ok, so it's in the vault. As a consumer **how do you react?** Do you panic and rush out to the nearest Wal-Mart to snap up a copy before they're all gone. Naw.

Instead **you kick back and wait**. If a situation comes up in which you or one of your little ones really wants to see Fantasia, then you're going to have to do something. A real possibility would be to check out one of the streaming video services such as Netflix, Hulu, or even Disney's own web site to see if it's possible to stream Fantasia to your home television. If that's not possible, then your next step is to go to Ebay. A quick check shows that you can get Fantasia in any one of its multiple versions (Blue-Ray, etc.) at any time for about US$20.00. Maybe even less if you're willing to bid for it.

One other thing, now that consumers have become much more educated do you think that they are going to be willing to be **blatantly manipulated like this?** If you notify them that products that they might be planning on purchasing in the future won't be available, what do you think that they'll do? Sure you hope that they'll hurry up and purchase them, but perhaps you'll tick them off enough that they'll go out and find substitutes. If I can't watch that Fantasia movie, maybe I'll go out and buy "Ice Age" (a movie from another film studio) because it's not in any silly old vault…

What All Of This Means For You

As a product manager I'm committed to preventing my customers from making a bad product decision. However, should I also be steering them to make the decision to buy now instead of waiting until later on? As product managers we can easily fall in love with **the concept of a product vault**. I mean, what's not to love?

The vault concept is pretty simple – **you artificially create a scarcity for your customers** and you let them know that it's coming so that they are motivated to buy now instead of putting a purchase off for the future. The problem with this concept is that with the arrival of Ebay and the digitalization of everything, this idea of making things scarce may no longer work.

As product managers we are responsible for making our customers **want to buy our product**. The old ways of making things scarce are fading away. As we move forward we're going to have to make sure that the next version of our product is so fantastic that there's no need to put the current version into a "vault", the latest & greatest version is what everyone wants to have!

Chapter 5

Which Forms Of Social Media Should Product Managers Be Involved In?

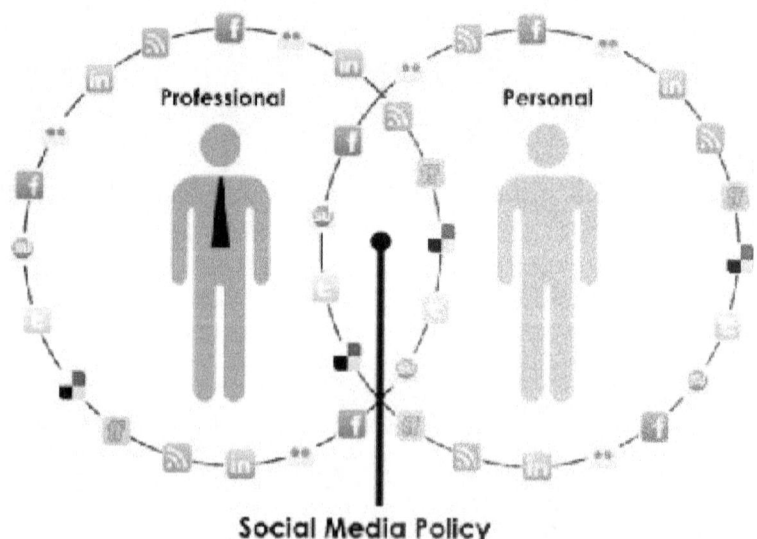

Chapter 5: Which Forms Of Social Media Should Product Managers Be Involved In?

How many **social media ecosystems** are out there these days? By my count (if you still include MySpace), there are 9 big ones. As an already overworked product manager working on your product development definition this means that you've got an important question that you're going to have to answer: which ones are you going to use to promote your product and which ones are you going to let fall by the wayside?

Picking The Right Metrics For Your Product

Before you can have any hope of evaluating which of the many different social media ecosystems you are going to want to pursue in order to promote your product, you are first going to have to make a decision regarding **which metrics** are the ones that you'll need to use to evaluate each ecosystem. Make the right choice and you'll have something that you can add to your product manager resume, make the wrong choice and there goes your product.

As you can well imagine, the list of possible metrics is quite lengthy. `However, the folks over at the Harvard Business Review in a recent study of the different social media ecosystems broke it down into **4 primary metrics**.

The first of these was, of course, gender. This was followed by age. Both of these may be critical metrics for understanding where your product's customers are spending their time. Next came education and household income. Taken together these metrics can **provide you with a good feel** for where the customers that you want to go after are spending their social media time.

The 4 metrics were then applied to 9 of the most popular social media ecosystems. These ecosystems included: **YouTube, Facebook, Twitter, LinkedIn, Reddit, Myspace, Pinterest, Google+, and Digg**.

Gender & Age

Where do boys and girls spend their time online when they are using social media? As you can well imagine, most of the social media ecosystems are fairly evenly split down the middle. However, **there are a few surprises**. Specifically, Pinterest is skewed towards the ladies with about 75% of their users being female. Likewise, both Reddit and Google+ seem to have more male users than female users.

When it comes to age, things get a bit more interesting. Not surprisingly, you are going to find **the older users using LinkedIn** as their primary social media ecosystem. However, this is followed by both Facebook and YouTube. The youngest users, those 24 and under, are the heaviest users of Google+ and Reddit.

Education & Household Income

When we dive just a bit deeper into the lives of our customers, we start to uncover more interesting things. The most highly educated users are using LinkedIn the most. The least educated users can be found on YouTube and Twitter. Across all of the various social media ecosystems, the majority of the users fall into **the "some college" camp**.

When we take a look at the role that household income plays in who uses what social media, once again **LinkedIn attracts the wealthiest users**. What's more interesting is that Digg is the site that attracts the users with the lowest income and this is followed by Pinterest.

What All Of This Means For You

The explosion of new social media ecosystems seems to be nonstop. Right now there are **9 separate popular social media systems** that some or all of your customers are probably using. Although social media was probably not a part of your original product manager job description, it's there now. There simply is not enough time in the day to stay on top of all of these different social media outlets so what's a product manager to do?

In order to sort through the various social media ecosystems, a product manager first needs to **prioritize which metrics** are the most important for his or her product. After that, analysis can be made based on gender, age, education, and household income.

The one thing that I think that we can all agree on is that the world of social media is still **rapidly changing**. Although we may never be able to be able to say that we are on top of it, with a little analysis we probably can say that we are spending our limited time in the right places.

Chapter 6

How Can Product Managers Get Sales To Use Social Media Correctly?

Chapter 6: How Can Product Managers Get Sales To Use Social Media Correctly?

By now just about every product manager knows that not only has social media arrived, it has just about taken over the world. The use of social media has made its way into everyone's product development definition. The problem that a lot of us are having is that we're not 100% sure about **how best to use this new marketing tool**. Where things get even trickier is when we try to figure out how to get our sales teams to do a better job of selling our products using social media. What's the best way to do this?

Guidelines

As a product manager, you need to realize that as your sales teams go out into the real world and start to use social media tools to interact with potential customers, **you may be facing a real problem**.

There are a lot of different things that your sales people can do that instead of helping your product to be more successful **may actually end up hurting it**. This list is fairly long but it can include such things as false representation of what your product can do, disclosures of unannounced features or pricing, and even copyright violations as they talk about the competition.

What's a product manager to do? You'd like to be able to add "knows how to teach sales to use social media" to your product manager resume, but how? The healthcare and the finance industry, because of how tightly they are regulated, have always had strict requirements about how their employees can communicate with the outside world. However, **confidentiality and privacy issues can pop up** in these or any industry.

What is going to be needed here are **some well-crafted guidelines** that show your sales teams what is permitted – and what is not. The good news for product managers is that there are companies that have already got this task done correctly: Nordstrom, IBM, and the U.S. Air Force are great examples. If you'd like to be able to have a good starting point for your company's social media guidelines then check out Chris Boudreaux's database of organizational policies.

Nuances

Just having your sales teams use social media is not going to be enough to attract more customers to your product. It turns out that there is **a right way and a wrong way** to go about using social media to sell a product.

There are a lot of **examples of the wrong way**. For example, in the world of social media your first impression carries a lot of weight and may be very hard to undo. The last thing that you want your sales teams to be doing is using social media like a modern day megaphone and shouting to the world how great your product is.

Instead, what you are going to want to teach them is to **personalize their social media messages**. Get them to participate in social media discussions often, not just every once in a while. Perhaps most importantly, you are going to have to teach them to provide lots and lots of value to the social media ecosystem so that when it comes time to sell your product, they have a willing and receptive audience.

What All Of This Means For You

There is no doubt that based on their popularity, **social media tools are here to stay**. That means that as product managers we need to figure out how to use them in order to maximize the sales of our products. If this isn't already part of your product manager job description, it soon will be. Since we don't actually sell our products, this means that we've got to find out how to teach our sales teams to use social media to sell more.

As with every new marketing tool, there are **a host of dangers** associated with these new social media tools. Before anyone goes crazy with them, it is your job as product manager to make sure that the company provides its sales teams with guidelines that will teach them what they can and cannot do. Once that's taken care of, the more delicate task of teaching social media nuances needs to occur if your sales teams are to be successful.

Social media is too important to be ignored by you – it's where your customers are living and interacting every day. Since it's your sales teams that will be selling your product, they need to learn **how to use social media to sell your product to your customers**. Take the time to teach them and you'll be able to count the new sales as they roll in.

Chapter 7

Product Managers Need To Know 4 Ways To Offer Their Customers A "Next Best Offer"

Chapter 7: Product Managers Need To Know 4 Ways To Offer Their Customers A "Next Best Offer"

What would **the perfect buying experience** with your product be for your customer? I'd be willing that it would go something like this. They'd contact you and explain their problem to you. You'd listen, and then based on what you already knew or could deduce about them you'd end up recommending the perfect product that would solve their problem. While you were at it, you might also suggest some other products that would solve problems that they didn't even know that they had. Too bad this perfect world does not exist...

What's Wrong With The Way That Your Customer Buys Today

When your customer goes shopping for a product like yours today, the experience is often not ideal no matter what you included in your product development definition. First, **they often feel as though they are alone in performing their shopping** – there is no sales professional who is going to help them to make their decision (sales people just try to get them to buy). Additionally, in a world with so many different product options, customers feel as though they have to do all of the work to determine which product / configuration is the right one for them. Clearly this is not something that you're going to want to put on your product manager resume.

The good news is that things are changing. Product managers are starting to be able to take advantage of data gathering techniques and analytics in order to create the ability to make the offer of the right product at the right price to their customer at the right time. This technique is called **making a "next best offer"**. In order to do it, product managers need to follow a simple 4-step process.

NBO Step 1: Define Objectives

It may sound silly, but before you can put together the right offer for the right customer you first have to decide **what your objectives as a product manager are**. There are a number to choose from: increased revenues, more customer loyalty, new customers or more market share? In addition to making sure that you know what your objective is, you are also going to have to remain flexible. When you start to get feedback from your customers, you'll need to be open to changing your objectives to better match what your customers want from you.

NBO Step 2: Gather Data

Once again, gathering data seems like it is easy to do; however, it turns out that you are going to want **very specific types of data**. This is going to include collecting data about your customers, your product offerings, and the circumstances under which your customers will be making their purchases.

Customer data will include such items as age, gender, income, etc. The customer data that you are going to want to collect now includes additional data items. This new information goes by the acronym SoLoMo: social, location, and mobile.

Your product offerings need to be known and understood in terms of **how your customers are going to be viewing them**.

You need to understand this so that you know how to make the best offer to your customers. Creating a good classification system for your products is the right way to start.

Finally, you need to understand the circumstances under which your customer **may purchase your product**. Which channel will they be using? Will face-to-face contact be required? Additional factors such as the weather and the time of day may also have to be factored in.

NBO Step 3: Analyze And Execute

Now that you have your data, it's time to analyze it and then start to use it **to create custom offers for your customers**. The simplest way to do this is to use a customer's history of past purchases in order to make recommendations about what additional products they might like to purchases. Taking this to the next level, you can use statistical analysis and predictive modeling to gage a customer's likelihood of responding to an offer that you present them with.

NBO Step 4: Learn and Evolve

One of the most important things to realize about making next best offers to your customers is that it is an inexact science. This means that each time that you are making an offer, you will be constantly improving both the offer and how you make it. Learn to view each offer that you make to a customer as **a test** and then take the time to observe the results of the test and adjust how you make your next offer based on those results.

What All Of This Means For You

Our customers are constantly being bombarded with sales and advertising messages about both our products and competing products. In order to help them to make their buying decision, the product manager job description now tells us that we must learn how to offer our customers **a next best offer (NBO)**.

In order to create an NBO for our customers, product managers have to follow **a 4-step process**. First, the objectives of making the offer have to be decided on – this will be important in determining how successful the program is. Next, data about your potential customers has to be gathered. At this point, the data has to be analyzed and matched to your customers in order to be able to make the correct offer. Finally, every offer needs to be viewed as being at test and the results of each test need to be studied and changes to the system made.

In order to prevent your product from falling further behind in the market, you are going to have to get good at this NBO stuff. Get started now and make sure that **you study the results of every offer that you make**. Once you master this technique it's going to be your competition that is struggling to keep up with you!

Chapter 8

How Product Managers Can Help Their Sales Teams Be More Successful

Chapter 8: How Product Managers Can Help Their Sales Teams Be More Successful

Product managers are NOT sales professionals. We pride ourselves on being marketing professionals and we don't think of ourselves as being a part of our company's sales team no matter how closely we may work with them. However, we do play a key role in the success of our sales teams and this is because they control how successful our product is going to be. This means that the big changes that are sweeping though the world of sales are going to change how we help our sales teams to be successful.

What's Changing In Sales?

In order for product managers to understand how best to help the sales teams that are selling their product, you first need to understand how the sales teams are going about selling your product. There is no great mystery here. Sales professionals have been using the same basic technique since sometime in the mid 1980's.

What they do is to what they have trained to do. First, they find customers who have a problem that your product can solve. Those customers who are getting ready to buy something get the highest priority from the salesperson. In discussions with the customer, the salesperson is looking for a so-called "hook" that they can use to attach your product to the customer's problem. Finally, the salesperson has to find an advocate within the company who will be willing to help then navigate the company's purchasing process and drive the deal to a close.

This approach used to work great – it was called "solution selling". However, times have changed. Customers are now showing up with a deep understanding of their own problems and are handing sales professionals a detailed RFP to bid on. The customer is now able to create their own solutions all by themselves (isn't the Internet a great thing?) All too often these days what this means for your sales teams is that they are transformed from solution sellers into price-driven order takers.

What Do Product Managers Need To Do Differently?

Clearly things have changed. Product managers need to be ready to step in and help your sales teams out. It turns out that there are three different areas where product managers can help their sales teams to be successful in the new world of selling your product.

The first is to change how sales people pick potential customers. The old way was to find a customer who knew that they had a problem that could be solved with your product. They would then find a "hook" that would allow them to attach your product to the customer's problem. Next they'd identify an advocate who could then help them to navigate the company's purchasing process.

In the new world in which we are living, you need to help your sales teams to identify customers who are agile. By this I mean customers who have the ability to act both quickly and decisively when they are presented with a solution to their problem. Old school companies that are buried in processes won't meet this requirement.

Next, you need to help then to find potential customers who are in what is called "a state of flux". We've all been there: a new acquisition has just happened, new management has just taken over, or perhaps some regulations that impact the company have just been changed. When this has happened, the customer will be more open to considering the types of product related ideas that your sales person can present them with at this time.

What Does All Of This Mean For You?

Selling your product has never been an easy thing to do. With changes in how your customers now operate, it has only become harder to do. The old way of solution selling no longer works because customers are smarter and they can build their own solutions given enough time.

Instead, what product managers need to do is to lend their sales teams a helping hand. You can do this by helping them pick the right customers. Customers who are agile and who can make quick decisions should be on the top of your priority list. Next, customers who are undergoing change for any one of a number of reasons should also be considered.

Selling your product is a hard job. Take the time to help your sales people pick the right potential customers to go after and you'll boost your chances of your product being successful. Their success will be your success.

Chapter 9

Product Managers Need To Learn To Think Globally

Chapter 9: Product Managers Need To Learn To Think Globally

Quick question for you product manager: does your product development definition consider **your product to be a global product?** Even if you said "no", I'd be willing to bet that if a big enough order showed up on your doorstep from some country that you had never heard of, you'd still try to find a way to get your product into their hands. Given all this, just exactly what does a product manager have to do if they are trying to make their global product a success?

What's Your Worldview?

As product managers it can be all too easy to spend our days thinking about our product and what comes next. When we realize that our product is now competing in a global market, we need to start to develop what is called **a "worldview"**. This is nothing more than having an awareness of what is going on in the world in which our product is being offered. Sure seems like this should be a part of everyone's product manager resume.

In the past our world consisted of such things as customers, competitors, and suppliers. When you develop a worldview, you now need to be aware of **opportunities for your product** that are showing up in different places around the world. This means that you are going to have to start to be aware of the forces that are active in the political, legal, and regulatory environments within the global markets where your product is being offered.

The list of things that you now need to be aware of **has suddenly become much longer than it used to be**. It's going to be things that can impact your product that you're going to have to stay on top of. This can include supply chains, basic infrastructure, capital markets, and even the quality of the local work forces.

How Do You Stay On Top Of What's Happening In The World?

Hopefully we can all agree that a worldview is something that every product manager now needs to both develop and maintain. This leads to the big question: **how are you going to accomplish this?**

As a basic first step, you are going to have to start to **pay a lot more attention to the news**. Being aware of what is going on in the world where your product is being sold is a new part of every product manager job description.

Your next step is going to have to be to **read publications** from those parts of the world where your product is being sold. There is no substitute for getting a first person understanding of just exactly how your product and your company are being perceived by the market in which you are trying to be successful.

One thing that you need to make sure that you don't do is to **ask someone else to do this job for you**. It can be all too easy to delegate the job of keeping up on the status of a global market that you are active in to someone else on your team – "… just keep me updated on what's going on." The reason that you can't do this is because it's important that you see how things are unfolding in your global markets yourself. Only by seeing the progression of events will you have a clear understanding of what the correct next steps for you and your product are.

What Does All Of This Mean For You?

Here in the 21st Century, no product manager can say that their product is not a global product in some way. What this means is that we all have to **adapt the way that we think about our product** in order to ensure that it will be a global success.

The first thing that we need to do is to **create a worldview**. This means that we need to be aware of things like changes in a country's political, legal, and regulatory systems. Once we've done this, we need to find ways to keep our worldview up-to-date. The best way to do this is to start to read local papers and magazines from the global areas where we want to sell our products.

The good news is that the market for a global market is much larger than products that are just sold domestically. The bad news is that in order for your product to be a success, you are going to have to change the way that you view the world. Take the time to do this right, and you just might have **a global success on your hands!**

Chapter 10

Product Managers Need To Know How To Find Customers In A Dark Room

Chapter 10: Product Managers Need To Know How To Find Customers In A Dark Room

Just exactly how much do you know about your customers? Sure, we all do some segmentation and stuff like that as a part of our product development definition, but do you really know where your customers are in terms of **thinking about buying your product**? Are they at the beginning? Are they almost ready to make up their minds? Wouldn't it be great if you knew where they stood and could take action to help them select your product?

Learn To "See" Where Your Customers Are

What all too many product managers don't realize is that our potential customers **don't see the world in black & white terms**. It's not like they are not our customers and then all of a sudden they are our customers. The act of choosing to become one of our customers is actually a process and this process is what we need to do a better job of "seeing" if we want to add understanding our customers to our product manager resume.

In the old days, it would be up to your sales teams to go knock on a customer's door and introduce them to your product. However, things have changed with the arrival of the Internet. Nowadays, our customers are taking the initiative and they are going out and **learning about your product using the information that is on your web site**.

What this means to you is that a potential customer goes from having no interest in your product to having some interest in your product via your web site. As a product manager **you need to become aware of them when this happens**.

With a little luck they will become more and more interested in the products and services that your company can offer to them. As this happens, they'll download more information off of your web site and perhaps will even decide to start a free trial of your product. All of these potential customer actions will help you to get a better view of where your customer is in their decision making process.

How To Use The Information That You Have In Order To Find Your Customers

I like potential customer information, you like potential customer information. However, the information by itself is going to do us no good. Instead, as product managers **we need to take the steps that are needed** to turn this information into knowledge that we'll be able to use.

What we want to do is to create tools and indicators that will let us know **where our potential customers are in their decision making process**. We want to know each time they log into our web site. If they are using a sample of our software, then we went to know when they run it. If they use an online calculator, then we want to know what they were calculating.

The value of all of this information is that it is going to allow you to **sort out your customers**. You'll be able to determine which potential customers have the best chances of turning into real customers and which ones are just "window shopping". With this level of information on how your potential customers turn into real customers, you can refine and shape both your product and their marketing message to help potential customers to reach a decision faster.

What All Of This Means For You

A product manager has many tasks to take care of. One of the most important of these is **knowing what his or her customer is thinking** – where are they in their buying decision making process. This task should be a part of every product manager job description. Our traditional sets of market segmentation tools won't answer these questions for us.

Instead, we need to start to take a close look at the clues that our customers are giving us about **where they are at in their decision making process**. In the 21st Century a lot of this has to do with the types of information that they are requesting from our web sites and how they are interacting with free or trial versions of our products.

Just collecting the data is never enough. As product managers we need to be sure to take the time to sit down and go over the data – **what is it really trying to tell us?** If you can get good at doing this, then you'll be well positioned to help your potential customers end up selecting your product when it's time to buy.

Chapter 11

Let Apple Show Product Managers How To Sell More Products

Chapter 11: Let Apple Show Product Managers How To Sell More Products

Is it possible that Apple might be able to teach you a thing or two about **how to find more customers for your product?** I can almost hear you saying "Hey Dr. Jim, I'm a product manager who manages a line of ball bearings – they are nothing like the kinds of products that Apple sells." Hold on for a minute there, sure Apple has a handful of very hot products, but how they go about getting them into their customer's hands has lessons for all product managers. Let's see if we can find out how they do it so that you will have something new to add to your product manager resume...

Say Hello To The Store

Apple is a computer company right? Well, no – they make a lot of money from software (their operating system and other applications) as well as that App Store thing. You'd think that they would be a perfect candidate for one of those companies that **"lives on the Internet"**. If you did, then you'd be wrong.

Apple has built an impressive set of retail stores that are very profitable. This kind of thing is measured by **revenue per square foot** and according to Wall Street Journal reporters Yukari Kane and Ian Sherr Apple's stores are able to generate $4,406 / sq. ft In comparison, high-end jewelry retailer Tiffany & Co. only generates $3,070 / sq. ft. How does Apple do it?

First off, the look & feel of an Apple retail store is not a fixed thing. As part of their strategic management of the Apple brand they continue to **change and evolve it** to meet customer's changing expectations. When you have a profit margin of 26.9% you can do things like this!

One of the key advantages of Apple's stores is **how they are laid out**. If you walk into a Best Buy store, you'll see that their products are organized by category (laptops, cameras, TVs, etc.). If you walk into an Apple store, you'll find things arranged by how you actually use them: kids, music, home, theatre, photo, movies, etc.

You wouldn't think that what you build a store out of would matter – I mean come on, we all shop at WalMart even though we know just how ugly those stores are. Apple took a gamble that what the store looked like **would motivate us to buy more**. They created retail stores that are very open and which sport a clutter-free look to them (no pallets of product sitting around). The store itself is part of the show when you visit: it's made out of natural materials such as stone, glass, wood, and just enough stainless steel. Take that WalMart!

It's All About The People Doing The Selling

As nice as the Apple stores are to both visit and to look at, when people visit the store **they have questions** and while looking at the complex products that Apple sells they may come up with more questions.

Apple realized from the start that the people working in the store were the ones who would control **a customer's long term impression of the Apple retail store**. That's why Apple takes the time to invest in their store employees.

New employees work with experienced employees right off the bat in order to learn how to interact with customers. This can take up to a couple of weeks. In order to make sure that their employees don't appear to be pressuring customers to buy products, Apple retail store employees **have no sales quotas** and receive no sales commissions if a customer buys a product.

Apple has gone the extra step and has equipped its employees **with scripts** that tell them what to say in different situations. Employees are instructed to not talk about product rumors and technicians are instructed to listen to customers explain their problems and respond with an "I understand" while listening.

What All Of This Means For You

Seemingly overnight Apple has apparently **reinvented the retail channel** for selling products directly to customers. Product managers everywhere can learn some important lessons from how Apple has done this no matter what kind of product you manage.

Apple has gone to great pains to ensure that their stores allow their products to be presented to potential customers **in the best way possible**. This means that they've considered all of the details that go into what a customer's experience is so that it all turns into a positive event. They also take the time to both train their staff to be helpful while at the same time carefully scripting what they say so that no selling opportunities are missed.

All too often we product managers tend to follow the other firms in our industry. We are content to interact with our customers **in the same way that they do** because doing anything different was never in our product manager job description. We can't continue to do this. Perhaps it's time to take an account manager or business development manager at your company aside and have a talk with them. Tell them that your company needs to take a cue from Apple and apply the retail store techniques that they've invented to your product in order to make it even more successful!

Chapter 12

What Sequestration Means To Product Managers

Chapter 12: What Sequestration Means To Product Managers

Sequestration is a big word that most of us are not familiar with. However, as product managers we should know it very well. What it refers to is when one of your customers decides to make across-the-board budget cuts. Sure they might be a great customer now, but when each one of their budgets gets slashed, what's going to happen to your product sales then?

How To Prepare For Sequestration

One of the most common places that you are going to run into sequestration will be **if your product gets sold to a government**. They are always running into budget issues and have to make cuts. Sorry, even the best product development definition can't anticipate something like this happening. However, should there be another global financial crisis then there is a good chance that any one of your existing customers might end up introducing you to sequestration.

As a product manager, you need to **anticipate this coming**. No, you can't prevent it; however, you sure can prepare for it. Do this well and you'll have something to add to your product manager resume. There's not just one thing that you can do, but rather a series of steps that you need to take in order to be ready for day when it arrives. Here is what you need to be doing.

Get Active: Every industry has its own set of associations. You need to make sure that your business is an active member of all of the associations that have members who might buy your product. What this means is that if your product is sold to larger firms whose contracts might get hit by sequestration, then developing contacts with other firms is what you need to be doing now.

Diversity Your Customer Base: Having all of your eggs in one basket is never a good idea. What you need to do is to take a long, hard look at just exactly what market segment your current customers are in. If it turns out that they all belong to the same segment (e.g. defense, healthcare, finance, etc.) then you had better get busy reaching out to customers in other segments in order to protect your product's sales.

Move Faster: We all have plans to grow our products. However, all too often those plans are off somewhere in the future. Since we can't control when a sequestration might happen, in order to prepare for the future what we need to do is to move faster. We need to expand our products into new markets NOW instead of later on.

Improve Your Internal Processes: How successful you are going to be when you try to go after new markets and target new segments of customers is going to come down to how efficiently your product team is able to move. In order to prepare for a coming sequestration you are going to need to take the time to optimize your processes so that you'll be ready to move quickly.

What All Of This Means For You

Just when you think that you have everything under control as it relates to your product, **a sequestration can occur**. Nothing in your product manager job description may have prepared you for this. That kind of across-the-board budget cut can cause even the best of products to go into a nose dive. As a product manager, you need to anticipate this happening and take action now.

There are a number of different things that **you can be doing now**. These include getting active in industry associations, diversifying your customer base, moving faster, and improving your internal processes.

There is nothing that you or I can do in order to prevent a sequestration from happening. However, there are a number of different things that we can do in order to **take proactive actions** in order to prepare our products before one happens. Take the time to sit down today and create a plan for the future. When the sequestration happens, you'll be glad that you did!

It's from the forge of failure that the steel of success is formed.

Hard Work Does Not Guarantee Success, But Success Does Not Happen Without Hard Work.

- Dr. Jim Anderson

Create Products Your Customers Want At A Price That They Are Willing To Pay!

Dr. Jim Anderson is available to provide training and coaching on the two topics that are the most important to product managers everywhere: how do I create the products that my customers want and what should I price them at?

Dr. Anderson believes that in order to both learn and remember what he says, product managers need to laugh. Each one of his speeches is full of fun and humor so that what he says "sticks" with everyone.

Dr. Anderson's Product Management Training Includes:

1. How can you segment your market?
2. What problems are your customers having right now?
3. Which of your customer's problems does your product solve?
4. How much of this problem does your product solve?
5. How much will it cost your customer if they don't fix this problem?

Dr. Jim Anderson presents over 100 speeches per year. To invite Dr. Anderson to speak at your event, contact him at:

Phone: 813-418-6970 or
Email: jim@BlueElephantConsulting.com

Photo Credits:

Cover - Jeremy Brooks
https://www.flickr.com/photos/jeremybrooks/2265352667/

Chapter 1 - Jacob Reyes
https://www.flickr.com/photos/90938583@N04/

Chapter 2 – bargainmoose
https://www.flickr.com/photos/31954284@N07/

Chapter 3 – Dr. Jim Anderson

Chapter 4 - Diefenbunker Museum
https://www.flickr.com/photos/diefenbunker/

Chapter 5 - Mark Smiciklas
https://www.flickr.com/photos/intersectionconsulting/4412472230/

Chapter 6 - Oceania Rock Radio www.Ocquo.com
https://www.flickr.com/photos/oceaniarock/

Chapter 7 - Satya Murthy
https://www.flickr.com/photos/inafrenzy/5787848646/

Chapter 8 – SalFalko
https://www.flickr.com/photos/safari_vacation/7496765660/

Chapter 9 - Wendy Cope
https://www.flickr.com/photos/litratcher/

Chapter 10 - !!!!jaZZed!!!!
https://www.flickr.com/photos/jaz_zed/4925175625/

Chapter 11 - MD111
https://www.flickr.com/photos/md111/

Chapter 12 – OzinOH
https://www.flickr.com/photos/75905404@N00/6094588003/

Other Books By The Author

Product Management

- How To Create A Successful Product That Customers Will Want: Techniques For Product Managers To Boost Product Sales And Increase Customer Satisfaction

- What Product Managers Need To Know About World-Class Product Development: How Product Managers Can Create Successful Products

- How Product Managers Can Learn To Understand Their Customers: Techniques For Product Managers To Better Understand What Their Customers Really Want

- Product Management Secrets: Techniques For Product Managers To Boost Product Sales And Increase Customer Satisfaction

- Product Development Lessons For Product Managers: How Product Managers Can Create Successful Products

- Customer Lessons For Product Managers: Techniques For Product Managers To Better Understand What Their Customers Really Want

- Product Failure Lessons For Product Managers: Examples Of Products That Have Failed For Product Managers To Learn From

- Communication Skills For Product Managers: The Communication Skills That Product Managers Need To Know How To Use In Order To Have A Successful Product

- How To Have A Successful Product Manager Career: The Things That You Need To Be Doing TODAY In Order To Have A Successful Product Manager Career

- Product Manager Product Success: How to keep your product on track and make it become a success

Public Speaking

- Delivering Excellence: How To Give Presentations That Make A Difference: Presentation techniques that will transform a speech into a memorable event

- Tools Speakers Need In Order To Give The Perfect Speech: What tools to use to create your next speech so that your message will be remembered forever!

- How To Create A Speech That Will Be Remembered

- Secrets To Organizing A Speech For Maximum Impact: How to put together a speech that will capture and hold your audience's attention

- How To Become A Better Speaker By Changing How You Speak: Change techniques that will transform a speech into a memorable event

- How To Give A Great Presentation: Presentation techniques that will transform a speech into a memorable event

- How To Rehearse In Order To Give The Perfect Speech: How to effectively rehearse your next speech to that your message be remembered forever!

- Secrets To Creating The Perfect Speech: How to create a speech that will make your message be remembered forever!

- Secrets To Organizing The Perfect Speech: How to organize the best speech of your life!

- Secrets To Planning The Perfect Speech: How to plan to give the best speech of your life

- How To Show What You Mean During A Presentation: How to use visual techniques to transform a speech into a memorable event

CIO Skills

- What CIOs Need To Know In Order To Successfully Manage An IT Department: Decision Making Skills That Every CIO Needs To Have In Order To Be Able To Make The Right Choices

- Becoming A Powerful And Effective Leader: Tips And Techniques That IT Managers Can Use In Order To Develop Leadership Skills

- CIO Secrets For Growing Innovation: Tips And Techniques For CIOs To Use In Order To Make Innovation Happen In Their IT Department

- Your Success As A CIO Depends On How Well You Communicate: Tips And Techniques For CIOs To Use In Order To Become Better Communicators

- What CIOs Need To Know About Working With Partners: Techniques For CIOs To Use In Order To Be Able To Successfully Work With Partners

- Critical CIO Management Skills: Decision Making Skills That Every CIO Needs To Have In Order To Be Able To Make The Right Choices

- How CIOs Can Make Innovation Happen: Tips And Techniques For CIOs To Use In Order To Make Innovation Happen In Their IT Department

- CIO Communication Skills Secrets: Tips And Techniques For CIOs To Use In Order To Become Better Communicators

- Managing Your CIO Career: Steps That CIOs Have To Take In Order To Have A Long And Successful Career

- CIO Business Skills: How CIOs can work effectively with the rest of the company!

IT Manager Skills

- Save Yourself, Save Your Job – How To Manage Your IT Career: Secrets That IT Managers Can Use In Order To Have A Successful Career

- Growing Your CIO Career: How CIOs Can Work With The Entire Company In Order To Be Successful

- How IT Managers Can Make Innovation Happen: Tips And Techniques For IT Managers To Use In Order To Make Innovation Happen In Their Teams

- Staffing Skills IT Managers Must Have: Tips And Techniques That IT Managers Can Use In Order To Correctly Staff Their Teams

- Secrets Of Effective Leadership For IT Managers: Tips And Techniques That IT Managers Can Use In Order To Develop Leadership Skills

- IT Manager Career Secrets: Tips And Techniques That IT Managers Can Use In Order To Have A Successful Career

- IT Manager Budgeting Skills: How IT Managers Can Request, Manage, Use, And Track Their Funding

- Secrets Of Managing Budgets: What IT Managers Need To Know In Order To Understand How Their Company Uses Money

Negotiating

- Use The Power Of Arguing To Win Your Next Negotiation: How To Develop The Skill Of Effective Arguing In A Negotiation In Order To Get The Best Possible Outcome

- Learn How To Signal In Your Next Negotiation: How To Develop The Skill Of Effective Signaling In A Negotiation In Order To Get The Best Possible Outcome

- Learn The Skill Of Exploring In A Negotiation: How To Develop The Skill Of Exploring What Is Possible In A Negotiation In Order To Reach The Best Possible Deal

- Learn How To Argue In Your Next Negotiation: How To Develop The Skill Of Effective Arguing In A Negotiation In Order To Get The Best Possible Outcome|

- How To Open Your Next Negotiation: How To Start A Negotiation In Order To Get The Best Possible Outcome

- Preparing For Your Next Negotiation: What You Need To Do BEFORE A Negotiation Starts In Order To Get The Best Possible Deal

- Learn How To Package Trades In Your Next Negotiation

- All Good Things Come To An End: How To Close A Negotiation - How To Develop The Skill Of Closing In Order To Get The Best Possible Outcome From A Negotiation

- Take No Prisoners In Your Next Negotiation: How To Start A Negotiation In Order To Get The Best Possible Outcome

Miscellaneous

- How To Heal A Broken Leg – Fast!: Understanding how to deal with a broken leg in order to start walking again quickly

- How Software Defined Networking (SDN) Is Going To Change Your World Forever: The Revolution In Network Design And How It Affects You

- The Power Of Virtualization: How It Affects Memory, Servers, and Storage: The Revolution In Creating Virtual Devices And How It Affects You

- The Internet-Enabled Successful School District Superintendent: How To Use The Internet To Boost

Parental Involvement In Your Schools

- Power Distribution Unit (PDU) Secrets: What Everyone Who Works In A Data Center Needs To Know!

- Making The Jump: How To Land Your Dream Job When You Get Out Of College!

- How To Use The Internet To Create Successful Students And Involved Parents

Tips &Techniques For Product Managers To Better Understand How To Sell Their Product

This book has been written with one goal in mind – to show you how to make sure that your product gets sold. We're going to show you how to work with your sales teams to provide them with what they need to sell your product.

Let's Make Your Product A Success!

What You'll Find Inside:

- **PRODUCT MANAGERS WHO WANT TO LOOK GOOD CAN LEARN FROM ESTEE LAUDER**

- **WHAT PRODUCT MANAGERS CAN LEARN FROM DISNEY'S PRODUCT VAULT**

- **WHICH FORMS OF SOCIAL MEDIA SHOULD PRODUCT MANAGERS BE INVOLVED IN?**

- **PRODUCT MANAGERS NEED TO KNOW 4 WAYS TO OFFER THEIR CUSTOMERS A "NEXT BEST OFFER"**

Dr. Jim Anderson brings his 4 college degrees coupled with over 25 years of real-world experience to this book. He's managed products at some of the world's largest firms as well as at start-ups. He's going to show you what you need to do in order to make your career a success!

www.ingramcontent.com/pod-product-compliance
Lightning Source LLC
Chambersburg PA
CBHW061158180526
45170CB00002B/855